MAYA ANGELOU

by Joyce Markovics

NORWOOD HOUSE PRESS

For more information about Norwood House Press, please visit our website at: www.norwoodhousepress.com or call 866-565-2900.

Book Designer: Ed Morgan
Editorial and Production: Bowerbird Books

Photo Credits: © DELORENZO/SIPA/Newscom, cover and title page; Wikimedia Commons, 5; Wikimedia Commons, 6; Wikimedia Commons, 7; © Ezio Petersen/UPI Photo Service/Newscom, 8; Wikimedia Commons, 9; © Shooting Star/Sipa USA/Newscom, 10; U.S. National Archives and Records Administration, 11; © Everett Collection/Newscom, 12; U.S. National Archives and Records Administration, 13; Wikimedia Commons, 14; Library of Congress, 15; Wikimedia Commons, 16; Wikimedia Commons/Allan Warren, 17; © olivier douliery/ABACAUSA.COM/Newscom, 18; © RG4/Ray Garbo\ WENN/Newscom, 19; Courtesy, William J. Clinton Presidential Library, 20; © face to face/ZUMA Press/Newscom, 21.

Copyright © 2024 Norwood House Press

Hardcover ISBN: 978-1-68450-670-5
Paperback ISBN: 978-1-68404-975-2

All rights reserved. No part of this book may be reproduced or utilized in any form or by any means without written permission from the publisher.

Library of Congress Cataloging-in-Publication Data

Names: Markovics, Joyce L., author.
Title: Maya Angelou / Joyce Markovics.
Description: Buffalo : Norwood House Press, 2024. | Series: Power of the pen: Black women writers | Includes bibliographical references and index. | Audience: Grades 4-6
Identifiers: LCCN 2023045979 (print) | LCCN 2023045980 (ebook) | ISBN 9781684506705 (hardcover) | ISBN 9781684049752 (paperback) | ISBN 9781684049813 (ebook)
Subjects: LCSH: Angelou, Maya--Juvenile literature. | Authors, American--20th century--Biography--Juvenile literature. | African American women poets--Biography--Juvenile literature. | Civil rights workers--United States--Biography--Juvenile literature. | LCGFT: Biographies. | Picture books.
Classification: LCC PS3551.N464 Z758 2024 (print) | LCC PS3551.N464 (ebook) | DDC 818/.5409 [B]--dc23/eng/20231002
LC record available at https://lccn.loc.gov/2023045979
LC ebook record available at https://lccn.loc.gov/2023045980

372N--012024

Manufactured in the United States of America in North Mankato, Minnesota.

CONTENTS

Introducing Maya........... 4
Early Years 6
Her Work 12
Maya's Power 20

Timeline and Activity.......... 22
Glossary 23
For More Information......... 24
Index..................... 24
About the Author............. 24

INTRODUCING MAYA

> "People will forget what you said, people will forget what you did, but people will never forget how you made them feel."

Maya Angelou (AHN-zhe-low) was a dancer, actress, teacher, and **activist**. But she is best known for being a writer and poet. *I Know Why the Caged Bird Sings* was her first book. In it, Maya told her own powerful story. She wrote about abuse and **racism**. Yet she also wrote about beauty and hope. "No matter what happens, or how bad it seems today, life does go on, and it will be better tomorrow," Maya said. She inspired people with her words. President Barack Obama called Maya "one of the brightest lights of our time." And her light still shines on.

ASK YOURSELF
WHY DO YOU THINK IT'S IMPORTANT TO BE HOPEFUL?

Maya Angelou wrote more than 30 books in her lifetime. This includes 5 children's books.

MAYA HAD A DEEP AND POWERFUL VOICE. WHEN SHE USED IT, PEOPLE LISTENED.

EARLY YEARS

> "Hate, it has caused a lot of problems in the world, but has not solved one yet."

On April 4, 1928, Marguerite Ann Johnson came into the world. She was born in St. Louis, Missouri. Her mom, Vivian, was a nurse and card dealer. Her dad was a Navy **veteran** and a doorman. Maya had an older brother named Bailey. He couldn't say *Marguerite*. So, he called his little sister "Maya" instead. Maya's parents fought a lot. When she was three, they got **divorced**. Maya and Bailey were sent to Stamps, Arkansas. There, they lived with their grandmother, Momma, and their Uncle Willie.

Maya was a tall child. She stood 6 feet (1.8 m) as an adult.

Stamps was **segregated**. Black people were forced to live apart from white people. Later, Maya wrote about Stamps. She said, "With its dust and hate and narrowness [Stamps] was as South as it was possible to get." Momma owned a small store. It was in the heart of the Black part of town. Momma was a strong and warm woman. She made Maya and Bailey feel safe.

Black workers in Stamps, Arkansas

SEGREGATION EXISTED IN THE SOUTH UNTIL THE 1960s. BLACK PEOPLE WERE MADE TO GO TO SEPARATE SCHOOLS, HOSPITALS, AND RESTAURANTS. IF THEY BROKE THESE RULES, THEY MIGHT BE THROWN IN JAIL—OR KILLED.

Willie valued education. He spent time teaching Maya and her brother. They learned how to multiply and read. Maya fell in love with books. Momma sometimes called her "little professor." Maya and Bailey grew very close. Sometimes, people made fun of Maya's thick, curly hair and dark skin color. This angered Bailey. He stood up for his little sister. Maya was grateful. "Bailey was the greatest person in my world," Maya said.

Reading became one of Maya's biggest passions.

> **"Any book that helps a child form a habit of reading... is good for him."**

In 1935, Maya and Bailey went back to St. Louis. Their dad wanted them to spend time with their mom. To Maya, her mom was a "pretty kite that floated just above her head." Like a kite, Vivian was out of reach. She spent a lot of time away from her kids. So, Maya often went to the library. She could spend an entire day reading. Maya said the books called to her, "Here I am, read me!"

Maya learned to read William Shakespeare when she was only a child.

ASK YOURSELF
DO YOU REMEMBER THE FIRST BOOK YOU READ? HOW DID IT IMPACT YOU?

> **If one has courage, nothing can dim the light which shines from within.**

Maya and Bailey moved in with their mom and her boyfriend. One day when Vivian wasn't home, the boyfriend touched and hurt private parts of Maya's body. She was only seven years old. Maya told Bailey. They cried together. Then Bailey told their mom. The boyfriend was sent to jail. But the police let him go the next day. Not long after, he was found dead.

As an adult, Maya would write about her difficult childhood. She believed her uncles killed the man who attacked her.

Maya felt she was to blame for the man's death. Maybe if she hadn't told her brother, the boyfriend would still be alive. Maya believed her words killed him. Only later did she understand that speaking out was the right thing to do. As a **traumatized** child, Maya stopped speaking. She didn't talk for five years. During that time, Maya read and wrote. "I memorized so many poets," she said.

Maya memorized poems by Edgar Allan Poe. Edgar is a famous American poet and writer who struggled in his personal life.

AS A CHILD, MAYA KEPT JOURNALS. SHE WROTE DOWN HER THOUGHTS AND FEELINGS. SHE THOUGHT OF HERSELF "AS A GIANT EAR WHICH COULD JUST ABSORB ALL SOUND."

HER WORK

> **"Do the best you can until you know better. Then when you know better, do better."**

Thanks to her love of reading and a friend's help, Maya got her voice back. In 1941, she moved to San Francisco with her mom and Bailey. Maya took dance classes. She began writing poetry and short stories. She did well in school. But Bailey hated school. And he didn't like being told what to do. So, he ran away from home. Maya felt broken. She left school too. At age 15, Maya got a job as a cable car **conductor**.

Maya enjoyed dancing throughout her life.

Knowing it was for the best, Maya went back to high school. In 1945, she graduated. Weeks later, Maya's life changed again. She had a child. The father was a neighborhood boy. Maya had to support herself and her baby. So, she worked many jobs. When she could, she read and wrote poems.

Maya became the first Black cable car conductor in San Francisco! She lied about her age to get the job.

ASK YOURSELF
THINK ABOUT A TIME IN YOUR LIFE THAT WAS HARD. HOW DID YOU OVERCOME THAT EXPERIENCE?

> **I'm convinced of this: Good done anywhere is good done everywhere.**

In 1950, Maya met Tosh Angelos, a Greek sailor. She married him. They shared a love of music. But the union ended in 1952. To make money, Maya took a job as a dancer at The Purple Onion, a **calypso** club. When she first went on stage, "My nerves shivered," Maya said. But she soon got past her fear. People flocked to see her. Every so often, Maya sang songs she wrote. Her talent led to a role in a musical, *Porgy and Bess*. Maya was overjoyed. She toured the world with the **cast**.

Before Maya became a performer, she changed her last name to "Angelou." She based her new last name on Tosh's.

After returning to California, Maya moved to New York with her son. In 1959, she joined the Harlem Writers Guild, a group of Black writers. But Maya was called to do something else. She heard Dr. Martin Luther King, Jr. speak. His words inspired her. Maya devoted herself to the struggle for **civil rights** around the world. Her **crusade** brought her to Egypt and then to Ghana.

ASK YOURSELF
WORDS ARE POWERFUL. HAVE YOU EVER BEEN INSPIRED BY WHAT SOMEONE HAS SAID?

Maya befriended Malcolm X in Ghana. He was an important civil rights leader. Malcolm was killed for his beliefs in 1965.

> **If you're always trying to be normal, you will never know how amazing you can be.**

In 1965, Maya returned to America. She went back to New York and wrote. Maya finished two plays and many new poems. One night, she went to hear Dr. King speak again. He asked her to work for him. She happily agreed. Then, days before starting her new job, Dr. King was **assassinated**. Maya crumpled. She sank into a deep **depression**. Her good friend and fellow writer James Baldwin helped Maya recover. He urged her to tell her own story. And she did.

Maya would borrow the title of her first book from a poem by Paul Laurence Dunbar. She found happiness while writing.

Maya then wrote her **autobiography**, *I Know Why the Caged Bird Sings*. She openly shared her trauma as well as her joy. She detailed her painful experiences and her **resilience**. The book was **embraced** by readers. Maya went on to write six more autobiographies!

ASK YOURSELF
IF YOU HAD TO WRITE ABOUT YOUR LIFE, WHAT YOU WOULD YOU SAY AND WHY?

Maya Angelou called James Baldwin her "friend and brother." James was a brilliant mind who wrote about race in America.

> **I am grateful to be a woman. I must have done something great in another life.**

Maya also published several books of poetry. Many of the poems were about the human spirit and being a Black woman in America. She said her poems were meant to be read out loud. "I write for the voice not the eye." Maya also acted. She starred in a play called *Look Away* and was in a TV miniseries, *Roots*. It was about slavery in America.

ASK YOURSELF
WHY DO YOU THINK POEMS SHOULD BE READ ALOUD?

With her booming voice, Maya held people's attention.

18

Oprah Winfrey interviewed Maya many times. They had a close friendship.

Maya also wrote a screenplay that was made into a movie. She was the first Black woman to do so! She traveled the country reading her poems and giving speeches. In addition, Maya took a teaching job at Wake Forest University. She adored teaching. Maya said, "I'm not a writer who teaches. I'm a teacher who writes."

MAYA IS KNOWN FOR HER SHORT, PUNCHY SENTENCES. SHE ALSO PAINTED **VIVID** PICTURES WITH HER WORDS.

MAYA'S POWER

> "If you're going to live, leave a legacy. Make a mark on the world that can't be erased."

In 1993, Maya read her poem "On the Pulse of Morning" for President Bill Clinton's **inauguration**. This was a first for a Black woman writer. Thousands of people listened with open hearts. Maya said, "You may trod me in the very dirt. But still, like dust, I rise." Her poem was a call for peace, justice, and equality. The crowd roared. President Clinton hugged Maya. "She was without a voice for five years and then developed the greatest voice on the planet," he said.

Maya at President Bill Clinton's inauguration

On May 28, 2014, Maya died peacefully at her North Carolina home. She was 86 years old. During her life, Maya was honored for her work. She won countless awards, including the Presidential Medal of Freedom. Yet what mattered most to Maya was bringing joy to others. "Try to be a rainbow in someone's cloud," she said.

ASK YOURSELF
LEGACY IS THE LONG-LASTING IMPACT OF A PERSON'S LIFE. WHAT KIND OF LEGACY WOULD YOU WANT TO LEAVE BEHIND?

Maya was always quick to laugh and smile.

TIMELINE AND ACTIVITY

April 4, 1928
Maya is born in St. Louis, Missouri

1931
Maya moves to Stamps, Arkansas

1945
Maya graduates from high school and gives birth to a son

1969
I Know Why the Caged Bird Sings is published

1982
Maya becomes a professor at Wake Forest University

1993
Maya reads her poem at President Clinton's inauguration

May 28, 2014
Maya dies at age 86

GET WRITING!

Maya Angelou moved people with her poetry. Select and read a poem by Maya. Then write a poem of your own in her style. Share your work with an adult or friend!

GLOSSARY

activist (AK-tuh-vist): a person who fights for a cause.

assassinated (uh-SAS-uh-neyt-id): killed suddenly for a reason.

autobiography (aw-toh-bye-OG-ruh-fee): a book about a person's life, written by that person.

calypso (kuh-LIP-soh): a type of music from a Caribbean Island called Trinidad with roots in African music.

cast (KAST): performers in a play.

civil rights (SIV-uhl RITES): the rights everyone should have to freedom and equal treatment under the law, regardless of who they are.

conductor (kuhn-DUHK-tur): a person in charge of a streetcar.

crusade (kroo-SEYD): a battle for change.

depression (di-PRESH-uhn): a serious illness that causes feelings of deep sadness and loss of interest.

divorced (dih-VAWRSD): no longer married.

embraced (em-BREYSD): accepted and supported.

inauguration (in-aw-gyuh-RAY-shuhn): a ceremony in which the president or other public officials are sworn into office.

racism (REY-siz-uhm): a system of beliefs and policies based on the idea that one race is better than another.

resilience (rih-ZIL-yuhns): the power to recover quickly from difficulties.

segregated (SEG-rih-gate-id): kept Black people separated from white people.

traumatized (TRAW-muh-tizd): experienced a terrible physical or emotional shock, or the effects of such a shock.

veteran (VET-ur-uhn): a person who has served in the military.

vivid (VIV-id): producing powerful feelings or strong, clear images in the mind.

FOR MORE INFORMATION

Books

Angelou, Maya. *Life Doesn't Frighten Me*. New York, NY: Harry N. Abrams, 2018.
Read one of Maya Angelou's poems with illustrations by the famous Black artist, Jean Michel-Basquiat.

O'Neill, Bill. *The Great Book of Black Heroes*. Sheridan, WY: LAK Publishing, 2021.
Explore the lives of 30 incredible Black people.

Websites

Britannica Kids: Maya Angelou
(https://kids.britannica.com/kids/article/Maya-Angelou/399338)
Learn about Maya Angelou's life.

Maya Angelou: Official Website
(https://www.mayaangelou.com)
Explore videos and read text about Maya Angelou.

INDEX

activist, 4
awards, 21
books, 4, 8, 9, 17, 18
brother, 6, 7, 8, 9, 10, 11, 12
childhood, 6, 7, 8, 9, 10, 11, 12
civil rights, 15

father (Maya's), 6, 9
grandmother, 6, 7, 8
I Know Why the Caged Bird Sings, 4, 17
jobs, 12, 13, 14, 16, 19
legacy, 20, 21
mother, 6, 9, 10, 12

poems, 12, 13, 16, 18, 19, 20
racism, 4
segregation, 7
Stamps, Arkansas, 6, 7
St. Louis, Missouri, 6, 9
trauma, 10, 11, 17

ABOUT THE AUTHOR

Joyce Markovics has written hundreds of children's books. She's passionate about celebrating the lives and accomplishments of women.

24